Miscreants

Miscreants

Poems

James Hoch

W. W. NORTON & COMPANY

NEW YORK   LONDON

For information about permission to reproduce
selections from this book, write to Permissions,
W. W. Norton & Company, Inc.,
500 Fifth Avenue,
New York, NY 10110

Manufacturing by Courier Westford
Book design by Lovedog Studio
Production manager: Anna Oler

Library of Congress Cataloging-in-Publication Data

Hoch, James, 1967–
Miscreants : poems / James Hoch. — 1st ed.
     p. cm.
  ISBN 978-0-393-06486-5
  I. Title.
  PS3608.O27M57 2007
  811'.6—dc22
                                        2007005201

W. W. Norton & Company. Inc.
500 Fifth Avenue, New York, N.Y. 10110
www.wwnorton.com

W. W. Norton & Company Ltd.
Castle House, 75/76 Wells Street,
London W1T 3QT

1 2 3 4 5 6 7 8 9 0

for Jeff Geib

Contents

Acts of Disappearance   13

Bricolage   15

Crop Circle   17

Sound of a Body Falling Off a Bridge   19

Angel of the Station at the End of the
Twentieth Century   23

Antarctica   30

Judith and Holofernes   32

Problems with Windows   33

Defenestrations   38

~

Bobby Almand   43

~

Late Autumn Wasp   87

The Witmer Boys' Attempts at Fainting
the New Goat   88

Leda's Aubade of Sink and Sledge   90

The Court of Forgetting   92

Morning After the Prom   94

Klutz   96

The Car   98

Plato's Aubade at Turkey Hill
Mini-Market   99

Blossom   101

Morphine   103

Draft   105

Underground Fence   106

Tree Planting   108

Painting of a Cart   110

All Things End in Fragrance   111

Acknowledgments   *113*

Notes and Dedications   *115*

Miscreants

Acts of Disappearance

It was a world where a moose
could pull a squirrel out of his hat,

children disappeared down holes,
and the lake outside your window

could suddenly go missing.
You sip your coffee and ponder:

abduction, subduction . . .

~

Freud said, when we look at the sea,
something like the sea opens in us—

which might explain Scully
drowning in himself or the night

Bobby didn't make it home, and why
I feel like a slick of mud.

Freud was talking about God,
not wax-winged punks shooting up

in a three-story walk-up, not a boy
building a fort— the hammer, the needle,

the report driven hellward.

~

It was a trick no one showed you—
how one could turn a lung into a lake,

a boy into air, carp on their sides,
the prevalence of sinkholes.

They keep asking for more;

the sea, of course, is not endless,
it only feels that way.

Bricolage

On the mantel split and pithed,
        held together by

a thick sheen, layers
      of colonial white,

      a ship's barometer
measures shift, stasis

      and for years was confused
for a clock.

     Above, the four of us
pose in photographs:

       headlock, prom dress,
motorcycle, uniform,
          a

      semblance,

  as
      our mother

stacks crossbeam,
            stud, wall—

primitive, room enough
        for a ball of paper, our faces

blossoming into ash.
            This is how

        you do it, she says,
            as if nothing
would turn us away.

Crop Circle

As if checking his own
    sobriety, my father, stepping

heel-toe, measured out
    a tetherball court in the center

of the yard, then, leaning
    on a ladder, hammered

a metal pole in the ground
    with the blunt side of an axe.

We thought he'd never leave.
    When he did, in a Cutlass

that seemed to steer itself,
    we took turns swinging,

ducking, our hands beet-red,
    the line whirling into knots.

Years wore the grass down,
    wore a bare circular spot.

If asked, we'd say: *Aliens*—
  A wild dog was chained there.

Sound of a Body Falling Off a Bridge

I can tell you there is no word for this
in any language. I've asked

and everyone seems to confirm
its translatability.

Feet shuffling off a stone pillar—
simple, but not easy. A young tree

fracturing under the sudden weight—
exactly how one imagines it.

And somewhere between shuffle and fracture
the silence of Scott Koch's body

falling off the Normanwood Bridge,
which is also the silence of stones

staring up from the riverbed,
where a swarm of mayflies

hatches in the predawn, coal-dark
aubade of a Susquehanna morning.

~

If you were a hatch of insects
or freshman in college

and bought some pot and drove out
with friends to gaze at stars

writing their arc across the sky
you would know stars make

a hell of a racket. Like time, like death,
they scrawl inscrutable marks

of light.

~

Say you are not a hatch of insects
or one of those kids wrecked and lovely,

their skins' leaf-awkward sheen.
Though if you were, you'd be lost

in a fury of living and dying.

You'll have to trust the words
for the way his face twitched, went

stone-white, for how unbeautiful
his body comprehended night,

for a breath not taken, for the arrested
air in his lungs. For anything else,

you'll need something like a life, or memory.

~

I give them to you piecemeal,
hand over hand, as if in aftermath

I press each against your mouth.
They taste of salt. They fall into place.

They are beginning to mean
less and less. They only do

what they do— cars ticking
over a bridge, wheel of a flower cart

knocking cobblestone.

Angel of the Station at the End of the Twentieth Century

When you think of silicosis,
you might imagine the faces of coal crackers

rising out of a mine in Pennsylvania
or construction crews working nights,

dense clouds of sawdust and drywall,
their bodies washed in flood light.

You probably don't think of Jim Scully
who, some claimed, wanted to be an angel

and having just spray painted *Fascists*
on the side of the high school, climbed out

his window, The Clash blaring over roofs,
and waited for his parents and the cops.

You don't think of Scully because Scully
stood for nothing, except himself, his sickness,

something in his blood, the wild misery
of not being able to be anyone but himself.

In History's geologic swell, it makes sense
not to remember Scully splayed out
on the grass, askew, the pale-wax
hide of his skin, the boy-fat,

pink-pudge of his cheeks, that smirk.

~

The claim that an invisible hand
garners exigence via an equivalency

with the hand of a butcher or bricklayer
seems disastrously flawed.

Although, looking at a leaf, bird, angel,
one recognizes the limits of self-definition,

that Wind and Gravity, Heat and Time
are certain as levers pulling

inside our heads, a vise closing,
as when we lay back on benches, twitching,

or noisily pace the terminal, waiting
for a train, a friend to arrive.

We call them *levers, vises,*
even though they are made of air.

~

Sometimes we call them angels,
as when Scully, wrecked on a mattress

in a shooting den off South Street,
laughing hoarsely through his phlegm-

slick throat, an arm tied off, a friend
sliding a needle into the groove of a vein,

waved his arms as if making an angel
in snow, his lungs like shallow pools.

It had nothing to do with angels,
though clearly they spoke to him

in the wispy manner you'd expect
from movies and bad paintings and Farrah

in the hormone-addled mind of a boy
who had tacked a poster of the feather-haired

actress to the ceiling above his bunk,
and spent late afternoons feverishly jerking

himself raw as if, having fallen so far
into his body, he would simply dust off

and fling himself back in the air.

~

I've never wanted to be angel or saint,
though I'd want Caravaggio to paint me—

exhausted, sullied, soil lodged
under nails, holding sheet music

for the boy, here, playing a violin
in the train station in Philadelphia.

Head cocked, he works his way
through an adagio, eyeing his case

and the destitute sprawled in pews—
half-nodding, half-begging, wheezing.

If you follow them into bathrooms,
stand at a porcelain trough spotted

with mucus and blood, and stare
into a length of tile, you can pretend

you don't smell or hear them
stroking themselves, the adagio droning on.

~

And you will not think of them
or the boy riding the train back home,

or the man wrapped in the arms
of a faceless angel lifting off the floor,

monument to Rail Workers, War Dead,
or the lungs of masons who carved

volutes in pillars, a schedule
of names in the granite base:

Anthony, Buwalski, Gulik, McKelvey.
And there, Scully.

What would I say—what would he—
if I could do something more than conjure him

simply by touching his name?

~

Outside, the sky lowers down
over the swollen Schuylkill, scull oars

feather the river. It takes us
sad or crippled, spared or perfumed.

It gives us back stone dust, flecks of metal,
knives in the fibrous lung, gives us

the disastrous breath, names, shards
flying back into place, the door

revolving, the station dissolving,
—whiteness, diesel—as we carry ourselves

in the littered streets.

Antarctica

Like nights we knelt on the dirt floor
of a dugout, leaned our heads back,
eyes twitching gone, and popped nitrous

canisters into the communion shapes
of our mouths, slipped inside where
everything seemed to be falling snow,

ice, the time split between chasing flies
through a darkened park and sprawling
in sycamore bark— how clean that abyss

we drifted in, like dew, more like pollen,
on our skins; and, beneath, a want
for touch, a kiss, a return. Like nothing,

back then, to break an arm latching on
to the bumper of an Impala, or settling back
as the car took us as far as the salted bridge,

before letting the ride go with a mitten
caught behind the chrome waving
from the other side of the river. *Like this,*

you said, sliding a needle, watching
dope plunge, the body's rush and tow
until you felt something like an angel

hovering above, but it was only pigeon
feathers deviling the air. Those friends
are gone: some dead, dying, locked up

or jailed in themselves; and when I see
some kids running in the heat of a taillight
swirling behind them, I remember we

wanted only to quiet our bodies, their
unnatural hum, a vague pull inward,
some thin furrows gliding over the snow.

Judith and Holofernes

In the dream—which is to say
    I felt; it gripped—my mother,

younger, a bombshell, white
    dress hemmed at the knee,

lords over my father's bed.
    He's sleeping the way

drunks do, content crashing.
    She has a pair of pruning

shears in her hand. Outside
    the shore house, the gray rot

of bay bottom mud. None of this
    seems likely, even in a dream—

my father *that vulnerable,*
    I mean—except the servant boy

standing beside her, squirming,
    apron held out like a basket.

Problems with Windows

Leave them closed, clear of curtains,
inevitably a sparrow ends itself

on the glass. You must imagine
how sudden everything is

for the sparrow keening away from a jay:
There's somewhere to go,

rectangle of light, glint, reflection,
then nothing. The bird

doesn't hear the thud of its skull,
twitch of its neck; that's for the air.

~

Leave them open long enough,
sparrows simply fly in. This one

must've tired of the heat beneath
the elms where young couples

grope in the shade under each
other's shirts before it shuttled

through the museum window hexed
with iron bars, and perched on

a light above Caravaggio's boy
holding a fruit basket, the way he looks

alone, almost burdened.

~

We had windows like that in a kitchen
I once worked, above a table

where we boned and skinned cases
of chickens that bobbed and thawed

in a sink, floating there, headless, wingless,
as if the birds had never been birds.

Shit can fly in, Franky would say, closing
the window, heat, and chickens in on us.

~

Franky, who was skinny but dangerous,
who lived by the river, had a knack for it

and, like Caravaggio, a penchant for blades.
You see, you had to break them open,

yank out the sternum, knife between
rib and tendon, leave no shard, then mallet

the meat until you could make out
the grain of wood beneath.

~

Nothing catastrophic happened.
The sparrow didn't crap on the painting

nor try to end itself in the shaft of light
behind the boy's head. It shuttled

room to room, passed Bernini's *Apollo*,
above the armless statues in the portico,

and out a window at the other end,
though such a rush, it felt torn;

which is to say, it filled me with memory.

~

Sometimes I look at a painting and forget
what to live for: the histories

perpetuated in the face of the boy,
or for the aloneness, the jitteringly nervous

suspension of a bird. I don't know
if Franky ended the way everyone thought.

The thing I remember is his eyes:
if they looked at you, shit was going down,

and if he stood still long enough,
they trembled like two dark pools.

~

And I imagine if you looked in the eye
of that sparrow, you would see the same

and a window of blue reflected
and curved and vulnerable

over its surface. Of course, to do so,
you'd first have to capture it, learn how to

hold a thing without crushing it.

Defenestrations

Tristan Egolf (1971–2005)

What sustains you when you forget
      your days barefoot in Paris,
wooing and begging, pawning novel
or guitar, or nights squandered
      dishwashing in Lancaster,

when you can't press your life in glass
      like a rare species of fly,
and can't remember what it was like
shoving fist and crowbar against
      a VW bus, a bottle into a wall

of bottles, nor remember the sound
      splintering, nor the dustpan
and sweep, nor the square of plywood
where you had set shard and sliver
      and polymered a windmill,

when you can't think of the elegant
      rigging of pirate radio
spitting Iraq and black-sacked heads,
and the beer and thong hugged hips
      of the Smoketown Six

stacked in a near naked pyramid,
        or how, as the motorcade
passed, and sprawled, cuffed
in the grass, a knee in your back,
        a lens caught you smirking,

when you forget Ralph Doyle
        heaving a cinderblock
then himself through the display case
of a bookstore storefront, lifting
        a mannequin, (*Reparations*—

he called them) only for the cops
        to follow a trail of parts
and find, huddled on an island
in the middle of the campus pond,
        Ralph rocking in his odd

unmedicated way the torso.
        Copper, Copper, never catch us . . .
(I heard Ralph married, has a kid.
Shane's back with The Pogues)
        What spell, what mocking,

what chant keeps you waking,
      when the pill and thorzine
drunks riding a late-night line
nod off or drown alone in
      the subway's ambient roar,

when you want to go with them,
      raft and river and rail,
want to lie down and sleep,
want to feign sleep like a swan
      or rat in a dog's mouth,

when you can't tell the taste
      of anything good
is courtesy, and love a vandalism
no restitution absolves,
      and forget how a song

—Tweedy, Elliot (*one's trying;*
      one had it hard, much
too hard)—can coil around you
and stay long like a patient snake
      wary of its own grasp,

like a sweet wandering note
        off Jeff Buckley's tongue
(*trees filled with gypsy moths*
when he went) when you tire
        of hollering over a field

of barn swallows careening
        in the freshly turned air,
of the barn air reeking lacquer
and turpentine, the alchemy
        of jars sealed by mouths

of friends who poured themselves
        down in, when you grow
suddenly sick of your own breath,
the stench of your sincerity, words,
        (*could we have said*

or failed to say, could we have
        crammed your life, left,
or leapt on the pile, listened . . .)
What sustains you when no longer
        a prop your boyhood

shotgun cocked against your head
        and the quiet won't quit,
can't take, being torn, when you are
about to make a window where
        there was no window, is this

swath of Pennsylvania gray,
        low-down February,
a diner, a plate of kasha
smothered in gravy, this girl
        in a plain Sunday dress

as she presses her mouth against
        the pin-holed end of an egg
and empties her lungs, this glass
clouded with paint, tulips, this waiting
        where your closure is not

yet steeled, your grief intimate,
        where you are and are not
what the world breaks against,
the wet hairs of a cheap brush,
        the bluing unfinished sky.

Bobby Almand

I

It is an awful sight— a horn
growing out of the head of a woman

preserved in a museum case.
And even as I squirm, contort

and marvel over the fingering
branch of bone, spur,

how it alters the rest—eyes
half-lidded, lips parted

as if to say something or have something
poured passed—I tell myself,

It's okay to look. It's okay to wonder
how the woman slept, took off

her clothes, made love, or answered
anyone crude or curious enough to ask.

II

A kind of permission the self grants,
the way Orpheus granted a plague

of arrows, the way our fathers ushered us
down the aisle at Blake's Funeral Home

where Bobby lay painted, perfumed,
neatly fitted in his baseball uniform,

American Legion stitched in cursive
over his chest. *Go ahead*, they said,

you can kiss him if you want.

III

When the neighbor kid found him
covered with sycamore

his jeans were unbuttoned,
his underwear *disarranged*,

pulled just below his hips,
pulled, they said, *back up*.

Someone must've gone to the trouble,
must've taken time, as if

after entering and leaving him
shirtless, facedown in a ditch,

it would've been indecent.

IV

Overnight,
        we acquired
the ethics of locksmithing

from a German who knew
        how everything worked
inside and out.

        The day-lock was
purposefully flimsy,

you can break in.

        After dark,
a different story,
        lost in our bunks,

        we had to be
certain, so he screwed

a latch for each window,
a dead bolt
        for each jamb,

except one. *In case of fire,*
he told us, *run next door*

and recommended dogs,
       and rigged a flood light

that turned the sycamore
bone-white and made

everything else
       seem darker.

Are you sure,
       my brother asked,
nothing will get us?

       For real?

*Football. He loved playing in the lot by Newton Creek.
To play he fought his mother, trusted his brother
not to rat him out. He had hair parted in the middle
and friends who thought he was good, stubborn,
mischievous. Like the rest, his father was not in the
picture. The picture hung over the neighborhood like a
pair of Chuck Taylor's dangling from a low wire. He
was good. He went to church despite fighting with his
mother. He wore a pair of Chuck Taylor's, religiously,
and loved playing football.*

V

There were two rivers:
One came from wealth,

somewhere far off and
wound under sycamore;

in winter we knew the ice
would not break, would

hold, and taunted us out.

One came from a hole
in the ground, and slowed,

a fetid stew; only a dare
or poverty could have you

swim or eating the catfish.

From the sky they were
lines of a palm: a mother's

worry; a father's lack.

From the sky, one was
for not crossing; one

for not drowning.
One for forgetting;

one for singing.

They were neither;
they were both; between,

we ferried our bodies.

VI

Like wild dogs, we were raised
     in packs, by packs,

and, early, had to be
     bound, reigned-in, heeled,

or our fate would be
     steeled in the headlights

of a Cutlass.

     Strong Force
   physicists call it—

when the smallest
     try to pull away, apart,

try and have to
     yield—

And, like dogs, we learned
     to love the leash

our master had to wield,
      and, wild, slipped

the collar, left
      our mother holding

the harness.

VII

The woods were called Crows,
named for either man or bird,

a smudge in sycamore, a stand,
a bluff overlooking Newton Creek

where we built a fort of stolen
lumber, stashed porn under foliage

and liquor bottles, tiny ones
because our mouths were small,

made of firewater, because
our bodies nearly leafed, like

the ragged heads of Molotovs.

Reader, what we did there,
would do, what cannot be said,

not fessed to anyone, we knew,
would burn, as would we

—one winter, still young,
out of school and out of booze—

for pouring buckets of paint
in the tanks of bulldozers

they used to clear the woods.
Nichtsnutz. When the cops

followed the prints we left
in the snow, and showed up

the next morning, our hands
still primed, we said

what Schultz always said:
I know nothing— nothing.

VIII

I wouldn't have let him go,
      his mother said, *but it was*

a snow day they hadn't used.
      Confused, she had that look,

as if she couldn't grasp what
      she was saying, summer snow.

The day my brother and I woke
      wicked, psyched, half-expecting

ice coating the sycamore.
      Slowly scorned, we measured

ourselves bowls of cereal,
      serial cartoons— Wonder Twins:

one shifted into a beast, the other
      water. *In the form of, form of.*

If we closed our eyes, tempting,
      the TV went on, flipping against

our lids, sirened, like the police
        plowing in the place of plows,

we could turn into anything.
        And if we left them open—window,

door—we were still there.

IX

If he were family, kin,
          I could understand

how a man might snap
the windpipe
               of a child,

bludgeon the skull
of an eight-year-old.

If he were *our kind*
it'd make sense to offer

          a boy on an altar
of sycamore.

          The Bible,
Star Wars said so, dumb
shows
          of backyard brawls,
Theater in The Hood.

But he was a *drifter*—
        as in stray, unmoored,

someone else's father
        some other's son,

a rumor the wind steered
        through our homes

until, one morning, the face
in the newspaper,

the name in the court record
        —Stannard—

he could say things.

X

It was his T-shirt
  tight and too small:

Mickey & Minnie
  Love is . . . I mean,

how could I resist?
  After that, simple,

rig a lure—a lost
  watch, a metal

detector—be kind.
  You think I am

a monster, maggot.
  You don't know shit.

So-called doctors;
  I've lost all faith.

That boy-smell,
  the thing I like

most, nothing
that tender, sweet.

Some young penis
swelling in my mouth—

cure that? Someday
you'll know, they do,

if it is so wrong, why
it feels so good.

XI

Everyone has a soul, our nun tells us,
      which, upon death, leaves the body.

Exspirito, she says, and when we
      don't get it . . . *as in exhale.* The one

who floats possumed in the pool,
      Possum Boy, lifts his head, smirking.

The one who sinks himself in
      the deep end, gripping the drain cover,

Drain Man, slowly lets out a sigh,
      breaking the surface of our boredom.

And a girl, too shy for any good,
      raises her hand and asks, *can a soul*

leap into someone else's body?
      Having seen the face of Jesus, our nun

is certain. Having swapped a few
      breaths of smoke, mouth to mouth,

we aren't so sure and look around
        the room, studying each other, each face,

waiting for Bobby's to leach out.

When he played football, he smiled. When he smiled,
his teeth showed and his eyes were unkind, narrow. He
had hair like a creek rat, got it cut at Sam's, like the
rest of us. He was small. He could eat a can of chips,
half a pizza, and a gallon of Coke in one sitting, then
play all hours in the park, even in winter, even on ice.
When he was cold, his teeth chattered like a bus pan.
He fell through the ice at least once. When he tackled,
he threw his whole body against you, anything to bring
you down.

XII

If I could draw a postcard: Collingswood, New Jersey,

early summer, circa 1977,   from the aerial of memory,

and send it back to you, boy   I once was, it would have the antique

silver, semi-clarity of sepia,   and two rivers slurring through

a grid of tree-lined streets,   alleys of brick homes, stenciled

mailboxes, names clipped   off the boat and a church

for every name, avenues of   half-empty fronts, ornate

displays, bouquets of dried   beef sticks in liquor store

windows lit in neon seraph.   If I could swing your head

like a boom, down, closer,   where you are standing outside

Sam's barbershop, the air   a toxic thrum: tonic, smoke,

swearing casual and thick,   and the cut hair, broom-stirred, floating in the slanted light,

magazines turned politely

unkempt in a row of chairs,

bowl cut, a wall of mirrors

so that they are ever-

descend, if you want,

the way Sam, who never

trimming a mustache

you'd see a stack of porn

facedown, and you sitting

waiting for a perennial

framed in a wall of mirrors

decreasing, so that you

and come back the same,

ages, plies a razor, just so,

back into a delicate line.

XIII

In the museum of the perverse,
in Mütter's turn-of-the-century

collection of elephantic scrotums,
cumuli of colon, gray hearts

conjoined and floating in jars,
they have a child drying

in an exhibit case, strung by
wire, drawn by wrist, like

he's levitating. What wasted
him was not clear, for years,

only that he grew rapidly old,
but tacked and splayed as if

being converted or slaughtered,
arms flung like that, how could

Christ or Icarus not come to mind;
yet cured, aged thin, the grain of bone

seems carved, Etruscan or, older,
the size of ones sunk in bogs,

woven in glaciers; though posed
like the dead in the tombs of Fayum,

you have to face them, have to
wait for a pure gaze, a figment

of soul, an image exact enough
the next world will know him.

Somehow the body keeps us
looking beyond form, keeps us

marveling over its hollows: empty
skull, depressed sockets—absences

we tend to, as we tend to narrative:
ash, grind, leaf, until he's only

a child again, selfsame—*Look,*
he's riding a bicycle, no-hands.

No, he's trying to hug the air.

XIV

Death too early wrongs the body.
You can see it on the face of this woman

who was simply born unlucky,
could've seen it, too,

on Bobby's face, if you knew him,
if you wandered in to Blake's.

Or if, years later, you are sitting
at The Manor Bar one Thanksgiving Eve

and his brother walks in.

You want to say something,
then realize and go back to drinking.

XV

You had to work, so you worked
a kitchen across from the woods

where they found Bobby's body.

Thanksgiving Special: all night
turkeys roasting in black pans,

pouring grease into pickle jars,
carrying them out to a dumpster

in the back lot. If one dropped,

smoke break: chef's whites
kicking on a stoop, Chuck Taylor's

grimed in fat, the opaque
windshield of an orange Dart

parked, clouded by breath, by bong,
hermit smoke and feather boa

roach clip hanging from a rearview,

and crows, slick-backed, pecking
at the macadam. You had to laugh;

their difficulty: shard and beak.

XVI

It goes away, comes back
　　　in pieces, in flakes of sycamore,

　　　　　　which has nothing to do with love,
　　　though it's ancient

for fig; *buttonwood*, shade tree.

　　　　　In a painting, a Caravaggio,
　　　　　　　a boy holding a fruit basket,

　　　　half-ripe mouth, leaf-loosed collar,
as if the face takes pleasure

　　　in corruption.

　　　　　　In a bar, someone makes a crack:
　　　That woman's got the ass

of a ten-year-old boy.

In my sister's voice
        when I walk into the bar she bought

                and drank in, and tell her I'm working
        on a poem about Bobby,

His brother was just in.

In bed, in memory, I picture him
        in his baseball uniform.

                In a news clipping,
                        Buried in his football jersey.

In sleep, then not, my wife asks
        what I am reading. *The news—*

                At Blake's Funeral Home

a boy in his baseball cap
walking away, stunned—

In handing her the clipping,
  I think this is me. In my hand

on her belly. In my worry.
In the son we may or may not have.

XVII

[If he had shut up, hadn't

                    whined his way out]

[If he watched cartoons

                    sunk in a chair]

[If he had been hungry,

                    can of chips]

[If he hadn't gone alone,

                    stayed so long]

[If it hadn't been summer,

                    Sunday evening]

[If he hadn't been

                    a peach]

[If he hadn't been so

                    eager, pleasing]

[If he allowed it, hadn't

                    resisted]

[If there was traffic,

          a light, some other boy]

[If he stumbled, stopped

          to tie his shoes]

XVIII

There are places we can not return from,
places we can not return to.

                                Seasons, cisterns—

Why go beyond, why forgive

                                what you are.
What was is done. Still, no dwelling.

No cyst of console.
No nesting

                         the tundra. Besides,

the firethorn's flaring
and your body

                      newly molted.

Quit your no good

                    mouth,
your yammering

                    wood blocks.

Leave a note of seed

                        silled.

Stay still, bunk-headed, coiled
into an 8-Track,

                and he'll come back

—as you like to think—a winter
        sparrow, not

        —as you know—
                a face with weight,
    elbow, knee,
        a son's

speech in the dark.

XIX

Someone to raise him out of a ditch,
brush the dirt from his face, carry a bag

down the slope of a hillside.

Someone to go numb awhile, not think
how little he weighs, walking into a ring

of news bulbs and onlookers.

Someone to set him down in a coffin,
powder and perfume, to shut his eyes.

Someone to not think at all.

And where there are stars ending,
and, not knowing their proper names,

someone to name them after

all the souls he had lost— one father,
a few friends, a yard full of dogs.

Someone to rage out of sleep, *It's my job.*
Someone to climb back in bed.

He was too small for football. The smallest, he had a brother, Froggy, who talked funny. He loved football, and his brother. His sisters smoked. Everyone smoked. He had a mother who was everyone's mother. He fought her every chance he could. He was too small to think about girls. Like a jackhammer, the way he thought about girls. He was kind, angered quick, indifferent often. In the school play, he made a good chimney sweep. He was too small. If you say his name, everyone knows who you are talking about.

XX

If you starve the eye of light,
bury it deep enough, sink it

in a cellar, cave, ditch,
the eye will feed itself a myth,

loose a false light, act as if,
as when I picture a seesaw

keeling in the sun,

and see two boys:
one older, the other

stranded in the air, pleading.

But if I think of the night
he went missing,

the all night uneasy sweep
of flashlights in sycamore,

there's only one boy

in the photograph— his brother
walking away.

I worry time makes small

slits in the iris, the sun
may some day

bleach the figures out.

CODA

If the white meant snow, it was snow
the man was leading his burro through,

the man made of faint blue marks
who could not be taken for anything else,

as the lines framing the winter scene
could not be anything but the mountains

of China, sprigs of pine, outcroppings
under which the man crossing a creek

perpetually crossed; even as my mother
packed a casserole with a hodgepodge:

leftover egg noodles, ground beef,
a can of mushroom soup that briefly

held the form of the can, crumbs—
even as she set the dish like a stone

down in the oven's black mouth,
the snow remained snow, the man

lingered stick-still over the creek,
the creek vanishing back into white,

and the dish, when it traveled the walk
from our house to yours, was still a cheap

import, ignoble, nothing more, what we
could give to you who had lost a son.

Late Autumn Wasp

One must admire the desperate way
    it flings
itself through air amid winter's slow
    paralysis

and clings to shriveled fruit, dropped
    Coke bottle,
any sugary residue, any unctuous
    carcass,

and slug-drunk grows stiff, its joints
    unswiveled,
wings stale and oar-still, like a heart;
    yes, almost

too easily like a heart the way, cudgeled,
    it lies
waiting for shift of season, light, a thing
    to drink down,

gnaw on, or, failing that, leaves half of
    itself torn
willingly, ever-quivering, in some
    larger figure.

The Witmer Boys' Attempts at Fainting the New Goat

A lemon perhaps or maybe deaf, the goat shakes
     his head,
wandering around the yard, unfazed, bored even,
     a primitive
mower munching the grass down to nub, certain
     sand, while
the boys in burlap and mud-up faces try leaping
     behind, try
hatchet wielding, banshee shrieks, and go on
     all day
trying, refusing to give in, a row of clocks
     lost in
a stubborn hour. The oldest hauls a mirror off
     the dining
room wall. The middle one, a monk or vampire,
     chants
Sleep Goat Sleep as the smallest gathers it in
     his arms.
Let's call him Baby Jesus he says. *In the name
     of Jesus,*
faint, he says, holding against his chest the goat,
     which is
neither fainted nor impressed, blinking, but ready,

nonetheless,
to be cradled in a world hell-bent on spelling him
into stillness.

Leda's Aubade of Sink and Sledge

Out of salt marsh, out of flat and reed,
out of crabgrass and black pine

they looked like swans
an archipelago of upturned sinks

dumped in a field. And I—
out of Meth, out on bail,

crank-addled, flannel-clad,
my punked-out throat slaked

threadbare—What made me
perch heel on wing above their necks?

Master, Miscreant—my body
buckling as I arched and wailed

a sledge into the porcelain birds—
I was what I heard looping in my head:

Anger is an energy. Mother,

I wasn't born as much as I fell out.
Mother, it's morning.

I don't know what's left to praise.
Your child's home, a blistered sun

tattooed over a sacral crest.

The Court of Forgetting

The awkward-gaited, the under-ripe
jacked-up over-jerseyed teenage boys
spill onto the court, a slab of desert
beaten in the yard of this way station
at the edge of the Reservation. The air-guitar
player, the air-baller, half-court rim-clanger,
the pimple-plagued conjurer of nipples,
the Bible-thumping believer that lingerie
carries the meadow-scent of angels,
they're talking trash, snatching loose balls,
laying them softly off the plywood.
The one who lobs piss from the overpass,
one who siphons gasoline, huffs hours
crumpled in woodsheds, in warm oblivion,
they're perfecting crotch grab and spit,
and got a mean pick-and-roll going on.
The one who pries his mother's fingers
from beer cans, one who wires pickups
and ditches them in canyons, one who
swaggers and stares stone-inducing stares
before crossing over and driving to the hole,
they have the sweet, easy hands, and pray,
if only briefly, for the clean, wet sound
of ball swishing net. The one who has taken

his uncle's prick in his mouth, the one
who showers with his sister, who lie in bunks
and weep as orphans and convicts must,
they are silence in the backcourt, deadly
from the perimeter. They are sly jukes
and dishes, cuts and pivots. They are all
sweat, hustle, break, forgetting minutes, hours,
deaths they've inhaled, that well in their lungs
and lift now off bodies acrid and salt-laden,
lifting like the dust, red and hanging in the air,
until someone calls time and they're done,
and everything becomes what it was.

Morning After the Prom

There was scrapple in the air
wafting out of Dempsey's Diner,
an uneasy quiet, part relief

part worry; even the crows
gossiping on the wires looked
fairly anxious, unnerved.

There was scrapple in the air.
There were corsages in the river
ebbing against the mill bridge,

a fabrication of things pale:
pink and white, ribboned in blue.
Perverted lotuses, soap opera

lilies, perfumed, starch-stiff
as shirt cuffs, and tied too
elaborately to break apart,

they floated and sank on
their own time. You can imagine
how the girls felt, slipping them

off their wrists, flinging
them into the water. You can
imagine their wrists, months

working a string of shit jobs
for a limo, a suite at The Oasis,
corsages in Kenmac's window,

and that moment, rehearsed
so well, even the music, the slow
grind of a heavy metal ballad,

how could the boys not
tremble a little, holding out
the flowers, so much going

away, so much coming on,
something they could talk about
the rest of their lives.

Klutz

Even the sound seems clumsy,
as if the word clogs the little space
between tongue and pallet, an accident:
shattering consonant, guttural vowel.
Looks funny, too, like a jogger with
a strange gait, or an animal that might
benefit from being run over, which is
about how he feels as she turns away,
retreats to her side of the bed and he lies
there, considering the error, the name
that just stumbled out of his mouth,
dumbly as the first time he asked out
a girl with blue spiked hair, a fragrance
of old pillows, and subsequent tongue
like an iguana. So he tries adjusting
the way he once tried puzzling together
a dish, a Japanese import from Hoboken,
shard and fingertip and Krazy Glue.
Bad idea, bad as wearing a white
pair of underwear on his head to school,
bad as taking that job as a pig inseminator.
Bad as climbing Normanwood Bridge,
bad as Scott Koch backing right off,
bad as reaching, bad as touching his shoe.

O heart, O George, O jungle. O God
fumbling for the light switch, here
is your awful toy, all sense tumbling
away from him as it does from you.
What else can he do but reach for her,
as if touch could fix a wrong, and coax her
hand and mouth back to bed, a skill,
the only one he ever had.

The Car

He liked the car because it went nowhere;
meaning, the car sat on blocks in the backyard
where rain fell relentless against old paint
and the living kept their clothes in suitcases;
meaning, slowly the car suffered erosion,
rust-weakened undercarriage, floorboards,
and the living talked of change, starting over;
meaning, some nights the car became a sofa,
where he nodded off with the agility of a drunk,
snoring away like a sympathetic engine,
and the living rented a room in a motel
with an unobstructed view of the highway;
meaning, the car was still there, in the yard,
when work went south and the house
sold to a young couple with fresh ideas
who hired a tow truck to haul the car away;
meaning the car was already in the junkyard,
stacked high on a cathedral of wrecks,
the stale rank of error, the heel marks of joy,
when he moved down the shore, where he rests
most days in a plaid, sagging chair, staring
at an unmovable ocean, his eyes like dull lamps.

Plato's Aubade at Turkey Hill Mini-Market

Stoned, I go into a gas station—
this is what I do—craving
something other than they offer,

and consider a sausage turning
on rows of steel rollers.

Morning Sausage $1.99,
though who can trust a sign.

I knew this Thai woman
who used to call a hot dog

Soul on a Roll. Ergo, I replied,
Who wouldn't want a soul?

She had a tattoo on her forearm.
Means Flower, she said. *It's ironic*.

It didn't last. I was in love
and couldn't shut up about it.

The sausage rolls one way;
the rollers another. Eternal, I think,

the form of everything left behind,

swath of blue shadow
over the eye of a counter girl.

Lily, the name tag says, *Lily*.

Blossom

Sometimes the break,
bound fist, compacted

green bud of a flower,
does not come.

Sometimes, a salve
for your eviscerations,

it leans against the lip
of a white bucket, plank

of wood, a corner stand,
and refuses.

Light coming on, petals
inward pressing, and all around

traffic, dogs
snapping at the wheels.

Even the grocer gives
a look, shrugs, then back

to his television,
where a cat's head

suddenly morphs
into a hammer,

and you stare back
at the flower, which

wants nothing to do
with you, your desires.

Morphine

The man lying in bed is dying
from cancer, flecks of bone
flow like ice in his blood.

Outside it's snowing,
lightly in the street, white petals
from a pear tree.

Everything is starting
to feel immense. His children,
like four pylons,

quietly resemble each other.
They pull at glasses
of Dewar's. They can't help

but notice the petals, the snow
blowing together in the street.
They chat politely, take salt

from his forehead,
on their lips, as they go
out the door, agreeing

he looks bad. They don't know
the man's floating on
a blue raft, an ocean, a small

Pacific. He's smoking
a pleasant cigarette; it's nice,
lukewarm, no undertow.

Draft

Some things, I knew,
                    were beyond choosing—
        father leaving, the endless

caring for mother, that love
        is a salving: what medics and nurses do.

Fodder,
                    I was too small to object,
        the conscription too severe.

So when you said
                    you felt *drafted*
        into marriage, the shudder

screwing up my face, you
        quickly followed, *just a metaphor.*

Try another I said, closing
                    the window,

drawing a breath between each
        sentence, trailing closely every word.

Underground Fence

You can see it on the face of a black Lab
      shaking
his head, as if he can't believe the new-
      fangled
device around his neck, puritanical, electric,
      stocked in

a twentieth-century collar that delivers
      a charge,
not enough to kill or inflict a visible wound,
      only a few
volts, *temporary* they say, *for its own good*
      as they stake

a perimeter of flags, something he might
      remember
when a bird or cat or child parades by,
      a voice
prodding: *No. Stay.* A jolt to say: *Boundary,*
      Property—

while he waits, peering out/in, hunger/
      affection,

as if waiting to receive a word, a hand,
    the next
sentence, as if about to leap into a bog
    of cranberries.

Tree Planting

Outside the hospital,
                they're planting
Bradfords along the sidewalk,
their roots bundled
                in twine, burlap.

There's no story here.

Through the traffic
                shovels clang
and scrape against frames of cement,
and the workers,
                covered in
Carhartt's, lift the saplings
off the flatbed.

They are still young—

the workers, the trees;
                everything shifts:

time, weather, the beetles who,
with their tiny scythes,
                      soon blacken
the blossoms.

Someone you love is dying.

It's the way it is— Like a thing
being set down inside,
                      you have to
take it.

Painting of a Cart

It's like some ancient machine brought from storage,
      another age,
and if it weren't selling imported flowers, you'd think
      the cart was
something you'd throw a few bodies on and haul
      through town,
regular enough its wheels warn of pestilence, poverty,
      reliable
as a church tower; and if you close your eyes and forgive
      the blossoms
the old stench might come wafting back, like a distant
      field feculent
and Dutch, spreading as the cart makes its way down
      the rancid
alleys, an odor thick as myrrh, slowly rising to a window,
      a kitchen
where you imagine you are chopping parsley, obliterating
      the leaves
into a stain of green; *how* you say to yourself, the wood,
      the knife knock,
the delinquent kids dragging a cart, clobbering the stones
      smooth with
their tiny hooves, *how could this have ever been*
      so lovely?

All Things End in Fragrance

Out the window, starlings
     fidget in the wasted eaves

of a bar burned down last summer.
They pilfer, figure,
          engineer

charred wire, booth cushion,
     anything light enough

to haul by beak, wedge high
     between blackened 2 × 4.

A nest,
     a bed for the dying
or just born—
        The birds shuttle,

their feathers taking on
     what they inhabit,

the way, Dear Witness, the silk
     in your shirts took asafetida,

mustard oil burning
in a skillet, as this letter

makeshift and late
receives
the leaden face of broken type,

a shape which, for now, says
Stay. Live here awhile

before rising into some other sorrow.

Acknowledgments

"The Court of Forgetting," *Rivendell*
"Antarctica," *Painted Bride Quarterly*
"The Witmer Boys' Attempts at Fainting the New Goat,"
   Carolina Quarterly
"The Car," *Pleiades*
"Draft," *Slate*
"Judith and Holofernes," *Gulf Coast*
"Morphine," *Black Warrior Review*
"Tree Planting," *Third Coast*
"Late Autumn Wasp," "All Things End in Fragrance," *New
   England Review*
"Painting of a Cart," *Virginia Quarterly Review*
"Sound of a Body Falling Off a Bridge," "Underground
   Fence," *Xconnect*
"Plato's Aubade at the Turkey Hill Mini-Market," "Klutz,"
   32 *Poems Magazine*
"Leda's Aubade of Sink and Sledge," *Ninth Letter*

I am grateful to the editors of the magazines mentioned
above for their kind attention to my work. To be sure, many

folks have helped my poems, but my utmost gratitude goes to Catherine Barnett whose caring and unsparing eye greatly helped this book. Heartfelt thanks to Rick Barot, Tom Sleigh, and Alan Shapiro for their support and to Beth Ann Fennelly, G. C. Waldrep, Major Jackson, and Patrick Donnelly and all my folk for providing guidance and attention. I am continuously grateful to the community of writers at the Bread Loaf Writers Conference. Special thanks to Jill Bialosky, Evan Carver, and everyone at Norton for taking on this project. I appreciate my friends and family for their belief in this work, especially Jeff Geib and my sister Valerie Fischer. Lastly, I am grateful for my son, who thrived in the shadow of this book, and to my wife for her love, patience, and trust.

Notes and Dedications

"Sound of a Body Falling Off a Bridge" is in memory of Scott Koch. "Antarctica" is dedicated to Joe Hershkovitz. "Angel of the Station at the End of the Twentieth Century" is for John Jablonski and in memory of Jim Scully.

"Judith and Holofernes" takes as its source a Caravaggio painting as does "Problems with Windows" which, at moments, nods to the work of Larry Levis.

"Defenestrations" is in memory of the writer and activist Tristan Egolf and dedicated to Jim Groff.

"Bobby Almand" was abducted, raped, and murdered in 1977, and in 1985 David Stannard was found guilty and sentenced to life in prison. Much of the italicized moments in the poem are direct quotations as they appear in newspapers and court records as well as the memories of family members. The poem is in memory of Bobby and dedicated to his family.

The Mütter Museum, affiliated with the College of Physicians in Philadelphia, boasts one of the largest collections of medical abnormalities in the United States.

Nichtsnutz: German; a preadolescent male, or slang for immature behavior.

Schultz refers to Sergeant Schultz from the *Hogan's Heroes* sitcom.

Wonder Twins was a television cartoon of shape-shifting superhero children.

Section XX involves the notion of "Dark Light" as it appears in *How to Use Your Eyes* by James Elkins.

The italicized lyrics in "Leda's Aubade of Sink and Sledge" are borrowed from Johnny Lydon and Joe Strummer.

"The Court of Forgetting" is dedicated to the staff and residents of Intermountain Youth Centers in Santa Fe, New Mexico, as well as to Sebastian Matthews. "Morphine" is for my sister, Valerie. "Draft" is for Marianne Sullivan. "Underground Fence" is for Carl Phillips. "Tree Planting" is for Joanne Sheaffer and Jeff Steinbrink. "All Things End in Fragrance" is for Michael Collier and in memory of Agha Shahid Ali.

About the Author

Poems by James Hoch have appeared in *Slate, Virginia Quarterly Review, New England Review, Ninth Letter, Pleiades, Black Warrior, Gettysburg, Five Fingers, Kenyon Review*, and other magazines. His poetry has been nominated for the Pushcart Prize, and his first book, *A Parade of Hands*, won the Gerald Cable Book Award in 2003. Hoch has attended the Sewanee Writers' Conference as a Tennessee Williams scholar and a John N. Wall fellow, the Bread Loaf Writers' Conference as a John Ciardi scholar and fellow, and the Summer Literary Seminars in St. Petersburg. He received a Pennsylvania Council on the Arts fellowship in 2002, and was more recently awarded a National Endowment for the Arts grant. In addition to his years working in social service, Hoch has taught at Franklin Marshall College, Lynchburg College, the Bread Loaf Writers' Conference, and the New England Young Writers' Conference. Hoch now teaches at Ramapo College and splits his time between New Jersey, where he lives with his wife and son, and Seattle.